CW00816431

TONBRIDGE TO HASTINGS

Vic Mitchell and Keith Smith

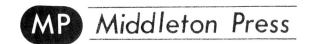

BRANCH LINES

BRANCH LINES TO MIDHURST
BRANCH LINES TO HORSHAM
BRANCH LINE TO SELSEY
BRANCH LINES TO EAST GRINSTEAD
BRANCH LINES TO ALTON
BRANCH LINE TO HAYLING
BRANCH LINE TO SOUTHWOLD
BRANCH LINE TO TENTERDEN
BRANCH LINES TO NEWPORT
BRANCH LINES TO TUNBRIDGE WELLS
BRANCH LINE TO SWANAGE
BRANCH LINES AROUND GOSPORT
BRANCH LINES TO LONGMOOR

SOUTH COAST RAILWAYS

BRIGHTON TO WORTHING
WORTHING TO CHICHESTER
CHICHESTER TO PORTSMOUTH
BRIGHTON TO EASTBOURNE
RYDE TO VENTNOR
EASTBOURNE TO HASTINGS
PORTSMOUTH TO SOUTHAMPTON
HASTINGS TO ASHFORD
SOUTHAMPTON TO BOURNEMOUTH

SOUTHERN MAIN LINES

WOKING TO PORTSMOUTH
HAYWARDS HEATH TO SEAFORD
EPSOM TO HORSHAM
CRAWLEY TO LITTLEHAMPTON
THREE BRIDGES TO BRIGHTON
WATERLOO TO WOKING
VICTORIA TO EAST CROYDON

STEAMING THROUGH

STEAMING THROUGH KENT
STEAMING THROUGH EAST HANTS
STEAMING THROUGH EAST SUSSEX
STEAMING THROUGH SURREY

OTHER RAILWAY BOOKS

WAR ON THE LINE
The official history of the SR in World War II
GARRAWAY FATHER AND SON
The story of two careers in steam

OTHER BOOKS

MIDHURST TOWN – THEN & NOW
EAST GRINSTEAD – THEN & NOW
THE MILITARY DEFENCE OF WEST SUSSEX
WEST SUSSEX WATERWAYS
BATTLE OVER PORTSMOUTH
A City at war in 1940

Design – Deborah Goodridge

First published July 1987

ISBN 0 906520 44 4

© Middleton Press, 1987

Typeset by CitySet - Bosham 573270

Published by Middleton Press
Easebourne Lane
Midhurst, West Sussex
GU29 9AZ
☎ 073 081 3169

Printed & bound by Biddles Ltd,
Guildford and Kings Lynn

CONTENTS

GEOGRAPHICAL SETTING

To the south of Tonbridge the route traverses the High Weald, an anticline, the crest of which has been eroded to reveal the Hastings Beds. These comprise alternate bands of Tunbridge Wells Sand, Wadhurst Clay and Ashdown Sand. These east – west bands, which have been frequently faulted, vary in resistance to erosion and so have formed the several ridges and valleys which made construction of the line very troublesome. The resulting route is therefore circuitous, with many tunnels and heavy earthworks. Steep gradients are encountered, especially on the climb from the Medway valley at Tonbridge and whilst traversing the valley of the River Rother and its tributaries. The varying hardness of the rocks has given rise to problems in the construction and maintenance of the civil engineering structures.

The economic geology of the area has also served the line. A small inlier of the Purbeck Beds is crossed near Whatlington, halfway between Mountfield Halt and Battle. Associated with these beds is a deposit of gypsum, which is mined in the vicinity and has given rise to a very substantial mineral traffic on the line. A geological fault crossing the route about ½ mile south of Wadhurst tunnel is associated with ironstone beds which were worked commercially in 1857.

All maps in this album are to the scale of 25″ to 1 mile unless otherwise stated.

ACKNOWLEDGEMENTS

We are grateful to the photographers and collectors mentioned in the captions for the assistance received. We also thank the Chalk Pits Museum, C.R. Crouch, Mrs. E. Fisk, Dr. T.A. Gough, J.A. Hodges, N. Langridge, J. Pennells, A.T. Raine, R. Randell, Mrs. A. Rose, N. Stanyon and our wives for the help given in so many different ways.

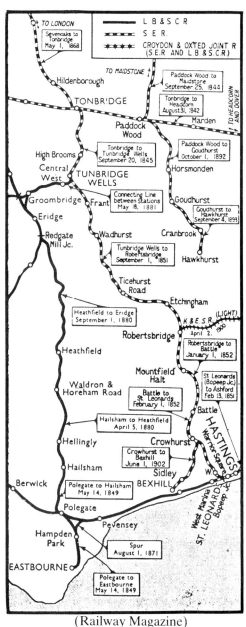

(Railway Magazine)

THE TUNNELS

The undulating Wealden terrain necessitated no less than eight tunnels on the route. Their history and effect on the operation of the line is worthy of special note.

Construction of most of them was difficult, owing to ground conditions varying from unstable clay to impenetrable sandrock which required blasting. Underground springs added to the problems.

The first major disaster occurred when 12ft of brickwork collapsed in Mountfield Tunnel in 1855. After this, other tunnels were checked and it was discovered that the contractors had failed to meet the contract specification. In Grove Hill Tunnel, the worst example, only one lining of bricks had been built instead of the four ordered. Moreover, no filling between the brick lining and the rock roof had been carried out. This is required in all tunnel work.

The SER took legal action against the contractor but their own resident engineer for the contract had, by then, left the country! The litigation involved Grove Hill, Strawberry Hill and Wadhurst tunnels.

There was no practical alternative but to add the three missing thicknesses of brick to the inside, thus reducing the already mean dimensions of the tunnel. Similar additions and ground movement has reduced tolerances in the other tunnels.

Despite this, further major repair work has been required, often necessitating long periods of closure. For exmple, Bo-Peep Tunnel had become so narrow by 1877 that trains were not allowed to pass in it. It was closed for six months in 1949–50 for a major rebuild, having been partly widened in 1934–35. Mountfield Tunnel was underpinned in 1938–39 when single line working was instituted for 47 weeks. Partial collapse in 1975 resulted in closure for six weeks.

As rolling stock became larger so restrictions regarding its use on the route became necessary. "Restriction 1" applied north of Tunbridge Wells and "Restriction 0" applied southwards, the latter meaning a maximum width of eight feet. In 1931, the SR introduced a special narrow version of the powerful Schools class 4 – 4 – 0 locomotives, together with a programme of special coach construction. The first-class compartments of the straight sided corridor vehicles sat only three people across!

BR decided that when this stock was due for replacement, a series of 23 six-car diesel-electric multiple units would be built for the route. These had short frames with straight body sides and were introduced in 1957.

HISTORICAL BACKGROUND

The South Eastern Railway's first main line ran from London Bridge to Red Hill, where it diverged for Reading and Dover via Tunbridge, the earlier name for Tonbridge. The latter place was reached in 1842 and on 20th September 1845 a branch was opened to Tunbridge Wells, but owing to the steep gradient at the junction trains proceeded towards Ashford for ½ mile and then reversed up a more gentle slope. Direct running was not possible until 1857. At Tunbridge Wells a temporary terminus, north of Wells Tunnel, was in use until 25th November 1846.

Operation was extended to Robertsbridge on 1st September 1851 and to Battle on 1st January 1852, Bo-Peep junction being reached one month later. The LBSCR had started to use the SER line from the junction into Hastings but a dispute arose, the farcical outcome of which is described in this section of the *Eastbourne to Hastings* album. The branch from the LBSCR terminal at Tunbridge Wells (later West) to the SER main line was completed by the LBSCR in 1872. It was used by SER trains initially, from 1st February 1876.

In 1899 the SER became the South Eastern and Chatham Railway and it was this organisation which opened a branch to Bexhill West on 1st June 1902. As an economy measure due to World War I, it was closed between 1st January 1917 and 1st March 1919. Final closure took place on 15th June 1964.

Frant and Stonegate were subject to Sunday closure from 1964 and to off-peak closure from 1966 until 1986. 1957 saw the introduction of diesel-electric multiple units on the route, to be superseded by full electricfication in May 1986.

When the DEMUs were in turn due for replacement, it was found that a timetable could be devised that would allow for four short sections of single track. Developments in signalling would allow them to be controlled, with automatic safeguards, from three panels, which would also control the whole route. Thus standard 9ft. wide electric stock could be used, following the provision of single track in the four worst tunnels.

Tunnel	Length (yards)	Date singled
Somerhill	410	Jan. 1986
Wells	823	Double
Grove*	287	Double
Strawberry Hill	286	Apr. 1985
Wadhurst	1205	Sept. 1985
Mountfield*	526	Mar. 1975

*Concrete slab laid by a slip form paver to improve invert stability. Rails secured direct to it.

PASSENGER SERVICES

Upon opening to Tunbridge Wells a generous service was provided, with eight trains each way on weekdays and four on Sundays. Evidently this was too much for upon extension to Robertsbridge in 1851 a more modest timetable gave just three trains each way on weekdays, one less on Sundays. Upon completion through to Hastings an extra weekday train was provided each way.

By August 1860, there were seven up and six down trains each weekday, the fastest expresses running between Hastings and London Bridge, via Redhill, in two hours exactly.

Any savings in journey time arising from the opening of the SER's cut off line via Sevenoaks in 1868 were offset by the westward extensions to the City and the West End, expresses reversing at Cannon Street before reaching Charing Cross.

During the latter part of the century, service frequency varied in detail from year to year and season to season. Typically, the winter 1890 timetable showed five fast and six stopping trains below Tunbridge Wells on weekdays and two journeys each way on Sundays; there were also three weekday trips south as far as Wadhurst.

The SER's "American Cars" brought a touch of luxury to travel over the route in the 1890's. Initially the six buffet and smoking saloon cars were placed singly or in pairs in various expresses but after 1896 they ran as one train formation for many years, being dubbed "The Hastings Car Train". In 1906, for example, they formed the 8.40 am up express from Hastings and the 3.35 pm down from Charing Cross; gentlemanly hours indeed in London!

By 1910, services had increased to 12 fast and 8 slow below Tunbridge Wells on weekdays, with four on Sundays. On weekdays, two of the trains operated to and from Victoria and there were two extra journeys to Wadhurst only.

After cut-backs towards the end of World War I, a steady increase in Sunday trains occurred, particularly in the summer, until there were seven each way in 1922.

The SR increased frequencies and by 1938, the weekday timetable showed (or shewed, in the SR spelling) 16 expresses and 9 stoppers, with 15 on Sundays.

Another World War brought further curtailments, the 1942 weekday service being four fasts and ten slows, with seven trains on Sundays. Post-war revival was slow, only two fast trains and three to Wadhurst having been added by 1948. The timetable for the end of the steam era provided nine express and nine slow trains on weekdays, with nine on Sundays and extras on summer Saturdays. Pullman cars were still provided in several of the fast trains.

After a transitional period in 1957, the full diesel-electric service came into use in 1958. It comprised a 12-coach train every hour from Charing Cross which was divided at Tunbridge Wells, the front portion (with a buffet car) running fast to Crowhurst and on to Hastings, whilst the rear portion called at all stations. On Sundays, the fast portion ran every two hours.

In 1977, a new timetable provided two trains per hour off peak, one stopping and one fast, the latter calling intermediately at Tonbridge, Tunbridge Wells, Battle and St. Leonards Warrior Square only. The fast services reached Hastings in an hour and a half, the slow trains taking 15 minutes longer. The enhanced service was only partially successful and the fast trains were withdrawn from January 1981. Buffet car services had survived until May 1980 when all catering facilities were withdrawn.

Electrification in 1986 brought some improvements, with a better service at the intermediate stations and a refreshment trolley service in a number of the trains, the trolleys have proved so popular that their use has been extended considerably in the May 1987 timetable.

TONBRIDGE

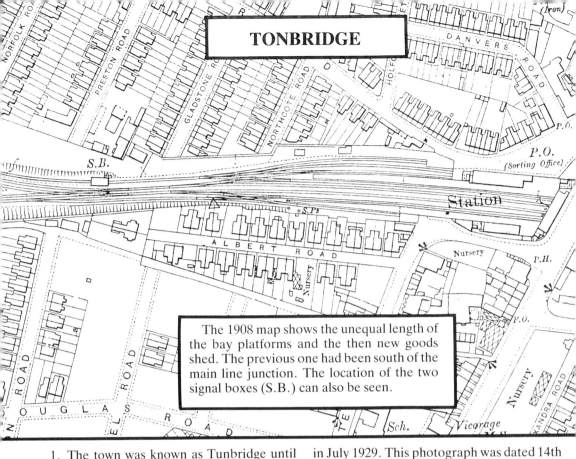

The 1908 map shows the unequal length of the bay platforms and the then new goods shed. The previous one had been south of the main line junction. The location of the two signal boxes (S.B.) can also be seen.

1. The town was known as Tunbridge until its offspring, Tunbridge Wells, grew so large as to cause confusion when letter sorting. The station name was changed to Tunbridge Junction in January 1852; to Tonbridge Junction in May 1893 and to plain Tonbridge in July 1929. This photograph was dated 14th September 1888 and shows the two bay platforms. The up bay, on the right, became a through platform when the station was rebuilt in 1935. (Lens of Sutton)

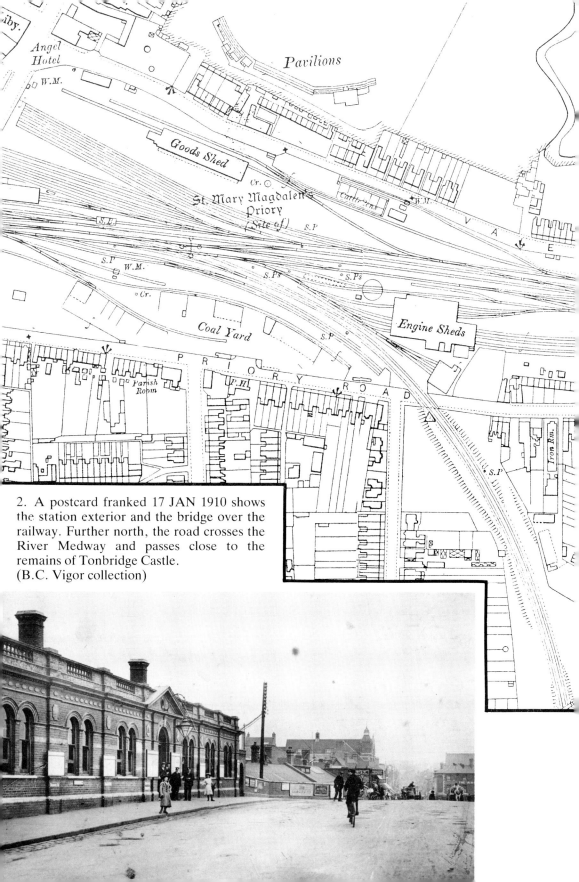

Angel Hotel

W.M.

Pavilions

Goods Shed

St. Mary Magdalen's Priory
(Site of)

S.P

Cr.

Carter Pens

W.M.

V
A
E

S.L.

S.P

W.M.

S.P

S.Ps

Cr.

Coal Yard

S.P

Engine Sheds

P   R   I   O   R   Y   R   O   A   D

Parish Room

P.H.

Iron Rm.

S.P

2. A postcard franked 17 JAN 1910 shows the station exterior and the bridge over the railway. Further north, the road crosses the River Medway and passes close to the remains of Tonbridge Castle.
(B.C. Vigor collection)

3. An eastward view from the road bridge on 15th September 1934 shows Schools class no. 905 *Tonbridge* arriving from Hastings. Behind the rear coaches, the locomotive shed can be seen and to the right of the Pullman Car, the base of the new East Box is visible. When complete, this box had 90 levers, nine of which were spares.
(S.W. Baker)

4. A May 1958 view westwards from East Box, by them officially 'B' Box, shows the rebuilt station and the additional bridge provided for the extra through platform. Trains from Ashford, Hastings and the coal yard could enter either up platform. Look at the plethora of point rodding. (D. Cullum)

5. 'A' Box can be seen at the top left, with the Sevenoaks line curving in front of it. Three coaches of a down train are visible in the station while empty coaches are shunted under 'B' Box. The east goods yard seems nearly full as six mechanical horses are busy by the goods shed. The locomotive shed, turntable and coal stage are to the right of the Hastings lines, at the bottom of the picture. (British Rail)

6. The 15.18 Hastings to Charing Cross service on 29th August 1985 was composed of two 6-car DEMU sets and is seen here passing the single electrified berthing siding. Car parks proliferated but the goods shed still remained standing in 1987. Industrial premises have replaced the locomotive depot. (J. Scrace)

7. The 2.38 pm departure for Oxted via Tunbridge Wells West attacks the stiff climb at 1 in 47 up Somerhill Bank on 10th May 1958. Behind H class 0–4–4T no. 31530 is the disused track bed of the indirect line, which avoided the steepest part of the incline. It remained in use until about 1913, although the direct lines had come into use in 1857. (D. Cullum)

8. Railway history is a blend of a variety of events. This is the first electrically hauled weed killer train on the route and is seen from the footbridge (shown in the previous photograph) on 16th May 1986. In the background, we see the North Downs and the modern junction signals. (J.S. Petley)

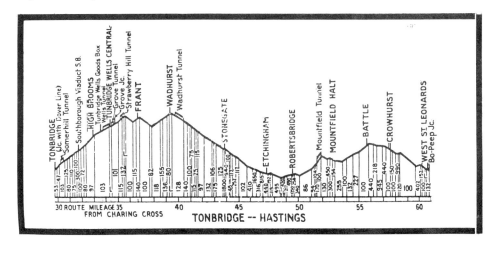

TONBRIDGE — HASTINGS

9. H class no. 31164 propels an Oxted train into Somerhill Tunnel on 24th May 1958. A mile south of the tunnel, the line passes over the 30-arch Southborough viaduct. Until June 1935, an intermediate signal box was located at the north end of it. (J. Scrace)

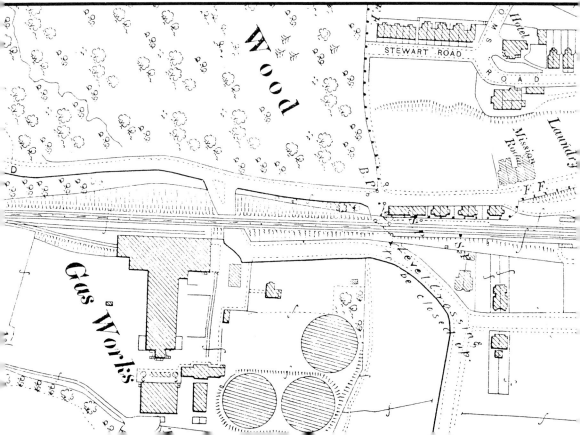

HIGH BROOMS

10. A northward view shows the staff and the station, soon after it was opened in 1893. Until 21st September 1925, the station was named Southborough, after a village one mile to the west. In the distance are the chimneys and sidings of the brick and tile works, also the signal box. (Lens of Sutton)

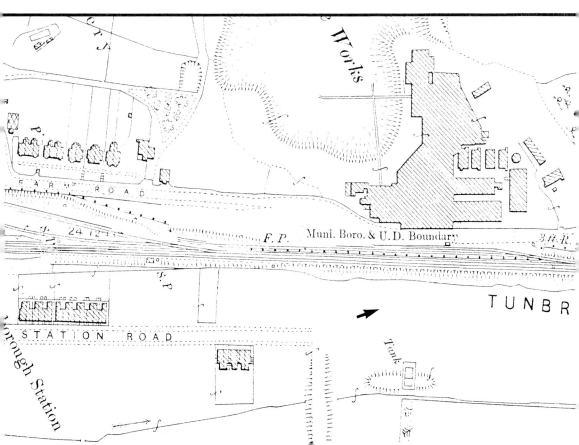

11. A view from North Farm Road shows the two short public sidings and the road transport of the era. Fortunately, the station remains largely intact in 1987, although the goods shed and dog kennels which feature in this photograph have gone. (H.C. Bassett collection)

12. Looking north towards the station in 1955, we see the gates of the Electricity Board's siding and wagons standing in one of the two Gas Works sidings. The latter is shown on the map. (D. Cullum)

13. No. 33206 approaches High Brooms on 15th April 1982, with a train of empty HAA wagons from Northfleet to Mountfield. The siding in the foreground is on the site of one of the former brickworks lines and now serves Wm. Cory's oil terminal. (J.S. Petley)

14. A 1985 photograph shows the detail of the up side buildings and how little they have changed since their construction. The curved roof covers the approach to the subway. The station was designed by a local architect and built with bricks from the adjacent brickworks. (J. Scrace)

TUNBRIDGE WELLS
CENTRAL GOODS

15. The former SER Goods Depot was situated half way between High Brooms and Tunbridge Wells Central, about ¾ mile from each. The last class I1X in service, no. 2002, is seen passing the sidings on 2nd July 1951, with the 6.9 pm Redhill to Tunbridge Wells West service. (J.J. Smith)

Features to look for on the 1897 map are the two separate coal yards, the Corporation Yard and the Electric Light Works. The latter was soon expanded and eventually moved to the site seen earlier, near High Brooms. The Grosvenor Road bridge was erected in 1883 and rebuilt in 1968 with lower parapets which permit easier railway photography.

16. The yard was busy on 10th May 1958, with some container traffic in evidence by the mobile crane. A fixed crane of 7-ton capacity was also provided. Two short sidings beyond the signal box were a late addition to the layout. The running lines are located under the smoke marks on the bridge. (D. Cullum)

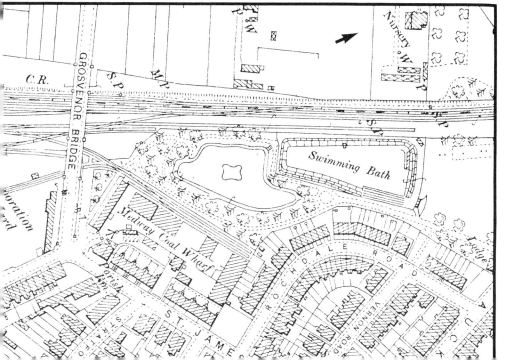

17. The yard closed in 1980 but a siding was retained for engineering purposes. Between 20th September 1845 and 25th November 1846, passenger trains terminated here whilst Wells Tunnel was being completed, the area being known as Jack's Wood Spring. Unit no. 1001 is seen forming the 11.43 Hastings to Charing Cross on 30th April 1986. (S.C. Nash)

Bradshaw 1910

LONDON, TONBRIDGE JUNCTION, TUNBRIDGE WELLS, BEXHILL, ST. LEONARDS, and HASTINGS.—South Eastern & Chath

Down. Week Days.

Miles from Tonbridge.		mrn	mrn	mrn	mrn	mrn	mrn	mrn	mrn	mrn	mrn	mrn	mrn	aft	aft	aft	aft	aft	aft	aft	aft	aft	aft
	228 CHARING CROSS ....dep.	5 15			7 15	8 6	8 25	9 10	9 30		1115	1120	1225		1 18	2 10			2 55	2 57	3 35	3 54	4 50
	228 WATERLOO JUNC... "	5 17			7 17	8 8	8 27	9 12	9 32		1117	1122	1227		1 20	2 12			3 52				
	228 CANNON STREET ... "	5 3 25	25		7 26	8 15	8 34	9 20	9 43		1125	1130	1231	1 23	1 30	2 20	2 32	3 3	3 45	4 0	5 0		
	228 LONDON BRIDGE... "	5 43	5 32		7 32	8 22	8 45	9 24	9 46		1129	1133	1239	1 27	1 34	2 25	2 35	3 8		4 5			
	228 VICTORIA ..... "									1030														
	Tonbridge Junction..dep.	6 45	7 25	8 8	8 33	9 8	9 40	10 8	1024	1128		1219	1 41	2 0	1 46	2 23	3 0	3 34	3 41	4 62		5 15	
3¾	Southborough	6 53	7 33	8 18	8 42	9 16	9 48	1016		1136		1 1	1 21	2 8	1 52	2 31	3 8		4 6				
4¾	Tunbridge Wells 196..	6 58	7 38	8 23	8 47	9 21	9 53	1021	1035	1140	1130	1230	1 17	1 32	2 12	2 36	3 14	3 46	4 34	4 57	4 10	4 37	5 20
7¼	Frant		7 43				10 2			1147		1 26		2 43		3 42	3 48				5 36		
9¾	Wadhurst		7 54				10 8			1153		1 33		2 49		3 48	3 54				5 43		
14¼	Ticehurst Road		8 3				1016					1 41									5 50		
18	Etchingham		8 10				1023					1 48									5 57		
20	Robertsbridge 174....	7 25	8 19				1030		11 3			1 55	2 22	2 29		3 56	4 15				6 10	3 26	
25¾	Battle		8 32				1043					2 7				4 8	4 27				6 16	6	
28	Crowhurst.........	7 39	8 38				1048		1117	12 51	9 2	13	2 48			4 32					6 20	6	
30¼	Crowhurst........dep.		8 38	46				1020		1121	1214	142	18	2 57		4 10	4 20			5 17	6 20	6	
31¼	Sidley	7 49	8 52					1026		1127	1220	202	24	3 3		4 16	4 36			5 21	6 26	6	
32¼	Bexhill ....arr.	7 53	8 56					1030		1131	1224	242	28	3 7		4 20	4 30			5 27	6 30	6	
31	West St. Leonards ...	7 46	8 46					1055		1123	1211	1 62	19	2 55			4 21	4 38		4 51	6 26	5	41
32¼	St. Leonards 180	7 50	8 50					11 0		1127	1215	1 22	2 23	2 59			4 25	4 44		4 55	5	5 1	6 23 6 27 6 45
32¾	Hastings 242 .....arr.	7 55	8 57					11 5		1132	1220	1 27	2 32	3 5			4 32	4 47		5 0	5 7	5 28 6 33 6 50

Down. Week Days—Continued. Sundays.

		aft	aft	aft	aft	aft	aft	aft	aft	aft	aft	aft	aft	mrn	mrn	mrn	mrn	mrn	aft	aft	aft	aft	aft
	228 CHARING CROSS ....dep.	5 25	5 30		5 36		6 10	7 20	8 8	9 43	1150	7 50	9 5	11 5			3 5		7 7	9 15				
	228 WATERLOO JUNC... "		5 32		5 38		6 12	7 22	8 10	9 47	1152	7 52	9 7	11 7	3 7		7 9	9 17						
	228 CANNON STREET ... "	5 35	5 39		5 43		6 19	7 30	8 20	10 0		8 0	9 12	1112	3 10		7 17	9 24						
	228 LONDON BRIDGE... "	5 37	5 43		5 48		6 23	7 37	8 25	10 3	1157	9 9	17	1118	3 12		7 24	9 29						
	228 VICTORIA ..... "		6 0							1030														
	Tonbridge Junction..dep.	6 10	6 24	6 36		6 55		7 38	8 41	9 40	1110	9 42	1030	1232	4 32		8 34	1046						
	Southborough	6 18	6 32			7 3		7 47	8 50	9 48	1118	9 50	1038	1241	4 40		8 42							
	Tunbridge Wells 196..	6 23	6 37	6 46	6 58	7 8		7 52	8 55	9 53	1123	9 55	1043	1246	4 45		8 47	1056						
	Frant		6 53					8 1		10 3		10 3			8 53									
	Wadhurst		6 58					8 7	h	1010		1010			9 4									
	Ticehurst Road							8 15				1019			9 12									
	Etchingham							8 22	1021			1027			9 19									
	Robertsbridge 174....							8 29	n	1030		1034	11 8		9 28									
	Battle							8 42		1036		1046			9 41									
	Crowhurst.........	7 14		7 34				8 48	9 38	f		1052	1122	12 5	9 59									
	Crowhurst........dep.	7 15		7 40		8 16	9 5	9 37		1045		7 25		1127	1210	5 18		6 10	9 53					
	Sidley	7 21		7 46		8 22	9 11	9 44		1052		7 31		1133	1216	5 22		6 16	9 59					
	Bexhill ....arr.	7 25		7 50		8 26	9 15	9 48		1056		7 35		1137	1220	5 26		6 20	10 3					
	West St. Leonards ...			7 41			8 56	9 40						1058		1212			9 55					
	St. Leonards 180			7 45			9 0	9 44	1048		12/8			11 2	1131	1215			9 59					
	Hastings 242 .....arr.			7 50			9 4	9 50	1053		1213			11 8	1137	1230			10 5					

NOTES.

a Stops at 9 22 on Wednesdays and Saturdays.

b Runs 12 later on Satur...

c Stops on Wednes and Fridays.

d Wednesdays or...

f Stops at 10 42 o Wednesdays Saturdays.

g Stops to set only.

h Stops when re to set down la London Passen

TUNBRIDGE WELLS CENTRAL

18. The station was opened on 25th November 1846, after the line had been extended from the temporary terminus beyond Wells Tunnel. A small locomotive shed is seen adjacent to Mount Pleasant Road, on the right. Note the road bridge on the extreme right and the hand shunting. (Tunbridge Wells Museum)

FEBRUARY, 1852.
UNTIL FURTHER NOTICE.

TUNBRIDGE WELLS AND HASTINGS BRANCH.

	WEEK DAYS.										SUNDAYS.			
Trains leaving	A.M.	A.M.	A.M.	A.M.	P.M.	P.M.	P.M.		P.M.	P.M.	A.M.	A.M.	P.M.	P.M.
LONDON BRIDGE at	7.30	9.30	11.30	...	1.30	...	4.30	...	5.30	8.30	6.30	10.30	5.30	8.30
READING	...	8.0	...	...	12.40	...	2.50	...	...	6.0	...	7.20	...	6.30
GUILDFORD	...	8.52	...	...	1.11	...	3.53	...	...	7.0	...	8.3	...	7.3
DORKING	8.5	9.39	...	...	1.58	...	4.0	...	...	7.40	...	9.0	...	8.0
Dover	7.15	8.0	9.15	...	11.45	...	2.0	...	5.15	...	6.50	10.0	...	6.0
Folkestone	7.50	8.5	9.20	...	11.50	...	2.5	...	5.20	...	6.40	10.10	...	6.10
Ramsgate	6.40	7.30	8.40	...	...	...	1.25	...	4.40	...	5.55	9.25	...	5.55
MAIDSTONE	8.20	...	10.25	...	...	...	3.10	...	6.10	...	7.30	11.10	...	7.0
TUNBRIDGE	9.24	11.24	12.36	1.41	3.21	4.3	3.10	...	7.24	9.36	8.24	12.24	8.3	9.36
Arrive at TUNBRIDGE WELLS	9.45	11.50	12.50	2.15	3.45	4.20	5.36	...	7.56	10.0	8.54	12.45	8.24	10.0
Frant	9.52	...	...	...	3.51	...	5.55	...	8.3	...	9.1	...	8.31	...
Wadhurst	9.59	...	...	...	3.58	...	...	...	8.10	...	9.8	...	8.38	...
Ticehurst Road	10.12	...	...	...	4.11	...	...	...	8.23	...	9.21	...	8.51	...
Etchingham	10.22	...	...	...	4.19	...	...	...	8.32	...	9.31	...	9.1	...
Robert's Bridge	12.30	...	...	...	4.31	...	...	...	8.40	...	9.39	...	9.9	...
Battle	10.45	...	...	...	4.37	...	...	...	8.55	...	9.54	...	9.24	...
St. Leonards	10.57	...	...	...	4.47	...	6.55	...	9.7	...	10.7	...	9.37	...
HASTINGS	11.5	...	...	...	4.55	...	7.0	...	9.15	...	10.15	...	9.45	...
Trains leaving HASTINGS at	7.30	8.0	...	...	12.0	...	...	...	5.0	...	6.0	...	5.10	
St. Leonard's	7.35	8.5	...	...	12.5	...	...	...	5.25	...	6.45	...	5.15	
Battle	7.50	...	...	...	12.20	...	...	...	5.10	...	7.0	...	6.0	
Robertsbridge	8.5	...	...	...	12.35	...	...	...	5.55	...	7.15	...	6.15	
Etchingham	8.14	...	...	...	12.44	...	...	...	6.4	...	7.24	...	6.24	
Ticehurst Road	8.5	...	...	...	12.55	...	...	...	6.15	...	7.25	...	6.35	
Wadhurst	8.38	...	...	...	1.8	...	...	...	5.8	...	7.48	...	6.48	
Frant	8.46	...	...	...	1.16	...	...	...	6.36	...	7.56	...	6.56	
TUNBRIDGE W. ...	8.55	9.5	11.0	12.5	1.25	3.0	3.45	5.15	6.45	9.5	8.5	11.45	7.5	9.5
Arrive at TUNBRIDGE	9.20	9.20	11.21	12.36	1.41	3.24	4.3	5.36	7.15	9.36	8.33	12.3	7.24	9.36
MAIDSTONE	10.25	10.25	12.25	...	...	4.35	...	6.50	8.30	...	9.25	1.25	8.50	...
RAMSGATE	12.10	...	...	2.30	...	6.10	...	7.30	10.10	...	11.10	3.10	10.10	...
FOLKESTONE	11.11	...	...	1.20	1.51	...	5.50	...	6.55	9.20	10.50	10.0	2.0	9.54	10.50
DOVER	11.20	...	...	1.30	2.0	...	5.20	...	7.0	9.30	11.0	10.30	2.30	9.45	11.0
DORKING	10.57	10.57	...	...	...	3.2	...	5.40	...	9.35	...	11.57	6.57	9.35	...
GUILDFORD	11.0	11.50	...	...	3.38	...	6.13	...	...	...	12.50	7.30	...	
READING	12.41	12.41	...	...	4.46	...	8.41	...	...	...	1.41	8.41	...	
LONDON BRIDGE at	11.5	10.50	1.15	...	4.30	...	6.0	...	9.15	...	10.20	2.0	10.15	...

19. The locomotive shed was replaced when through running to Robertsbridge commenced in 1851. A traverser can be seen in the foreground whilst small turntables were provided at this location in the previous view. A signal box stood beyond the coach until December 1928. (Lens of Sutton)

20. The grandiose architecture of Mount Pleasant reflects the opulence of the district which expanded following the arrival of the railway. The down side buildings and the footbridge roof are on the left. (D. Cullum collection)

21. The down side was rebuilt in 1911 and the clock was given even more prominence by placing it in an ornate tower. Until the SR added the suffix *CENTRAL* on 9th July 1923, the station was simply known as SER or SECR. The closure of Tunbridge Wells West on 6th July 1985 eliminated the need for a distinction. (B.C. Vigor collection)

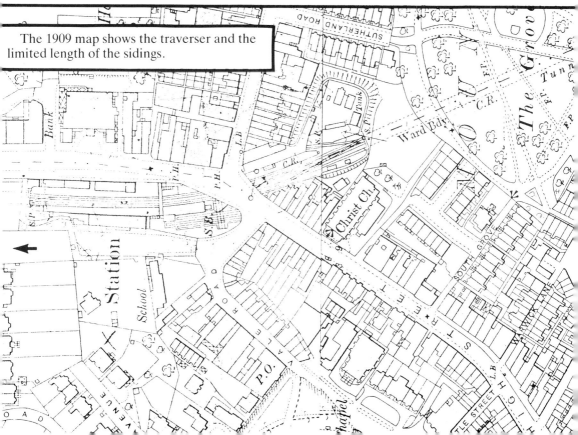

The 1909 map shows the traverser and the limited length of the sidings.

22. A photograph from 3rd August 1938 shows the wooden extension of the up platform and one of the Schools class 4–4–0s, *Wellington*, leaving for Hastings on the 1 in 101 up gradient through Grove Tunnel. (J. Turley)

SOUTHERN RAILWAY

(4/47) 24ᴍ   —————   Stock
TO   787

HASTINGS

SOUTHERN RAILWAY.

(2/46) 24ᴍ   —————   Stock
TO   787

TUNBRIDGE WELLS CENTRAL

23. The platforms were further lengthened
in 1957 to accommodate two 6-car DEMU
sets. One such set is seen arriving from Hastings in June 1980. The banner repeater signal
reminds us that earlier, during the final phase
of mechanical signalling, up trains were controlled by Tunbridge Wells Central Goods
and the down ones by Grove Junction, there
being no Central box. (A.C. Mott)

24. A 1986 view shows both up and down side buildings to have been well conserved and the coupled chimney stacks, much loved by architect William Tress, to have been retained, although the one on the left does not appear to be original. (V. Mitchell)

26. Diesel-electric traction returned unexpectedly to the route on 15th January 1987 when very severe weather conditions brought most of Kent to a standstill. No. 203001 (a 4-car unit, seen here), an Oxted unit and a Hampshire unit operated a shuttle service between Tonbridge and Hastings. (A. Ginman)

25. Since the advent of electrification in 1986, most down trains use the up platform, as seen here. The down side is used for terminating trains in peak hours and therefore does not have to be fully staffed. An additional shelter has been provided to the already generous cover. (S.C. Nash)

GROVE JUNCTION

27. The junction for the former LBSCR line to Tunbridge Wells West was ¼ mile south of the Central station. Class C no. 31725 leaves that line on 21st June 1951 with the 4.45 pm East Croydon to Tonbridge passenger service, which had been the rear portion of the 4.20 from London Bridge. The milk tanks had come from Ffairfach in Carmarthenshire, via Kensington Olympia. (J.J. Smith)

29. Photographed on the same day, this small box was far from being a peaceful country retreat, as at this time it handled over 100 trains per day. The box closed on 20th April 1986 and Strawberry Hill tunnel, to the south of it, was singled in April 1985. South of the tunnel a 15-lever signal box controlled entry to Forest Brickworks siding, from 1898 to about 1910. (J. Scrace)

28. The junction was at the southern portal of Grove Tunnel. In green livery, unit no. 1013 throbs through the southern suburbs of the spa town, en route to Hastings on 24th May 1958. (J. Scrace)

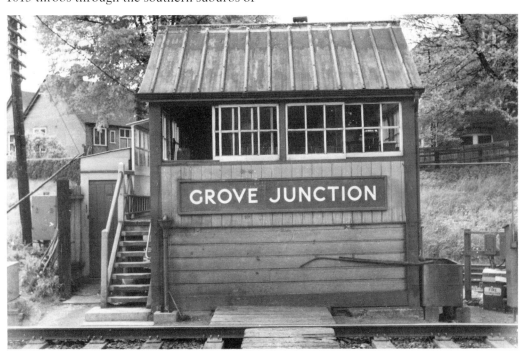

30. In its final years, the single line to Tunbridge Wells West carried a basic hourly service between Tonbridge and Eridge. The 13.35 from Eridge is seen joining the main line on 3rd September 1969. (J. Scrace)

Photographs of Tunbridge Wells West are to be found in our *Branch Lines to East Grinstead* and *Branch Lines to Tunbridge Wells*.

FRANT

31. This is the first Gothic style station on the line and comparison with the next photograph shows that it lost its bay windows. The minute signal box controlled the two arms on the single post. (Lens of Sutton)

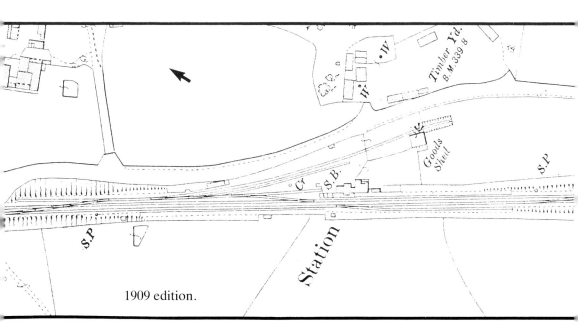

1909 edition.

32. The proximity of the new larger signal box to the down line is evident here. Look for the fine tracery in the brackets for the awning which was added in 1905, allegedly for the benefit of royal visitors to Lord Camden's estate. The building was also extended at that time. (Lens of Sutton)

33. The lack of symmetry and the two patterns of roof tiles add charm to this rural station, which is situated nearly 1½ miles from Frant. The line in the foreground of this pre-WWII photograph once led to the goods shed and to the Fernden Fencing Company's siding. (D. Cullum collection)

34. A view from the down home signal in 1955 shows the bridge over the B2169 in the foreground and the bridge carrying the road to Frant in the background. It also shows the pleasant rural location of the station, the small community largely hidden by the trees on the left being known as Bell's Yew Green. (D. Cullum)

35. The front wall of the machine room of the signal box was removed to improve visibility and clearances, following the death of a signalman in 1935. Another curious feature was the incision in the barge board for the stove pipe. As at Winchelsea, the sign *GENTLEMEN* was far more obvious than any other. (D. Cullum)

36. A view after the signal box was demolished shows a colour light signal at the end of the up platform and a semaphore unusually placed in the goods yard, as the down siding starting signal. A "Lifebuoy" feature was the incision in the barge board for the stove pipe. As at Winchelsea, the sign *GENTLEMEN* was far more obvious than any other. Tilley lamp hangs from the canopy and a set of steps can be seen by the wall. These were used to aid the less athletic passengers entering or leaving trains from the low platforms. (Lens of Sutton)

WADHURST

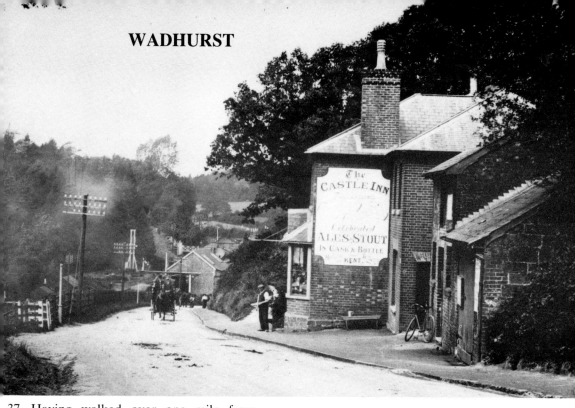

37. Having walked over one mile from Wadhurst, this was the passenger's view of the station. The white posts are the petrol gas producer which supplied gas for the station lighting until about 1945. The Castle Inn was later to become the Four Keys Inn. (H.C. Bassett collection)

The 1874 map shows two wagon turntables and a crossover line. They remained in use until about 1905 and they were controlled by bolts from lever no. 12 in their latter years.

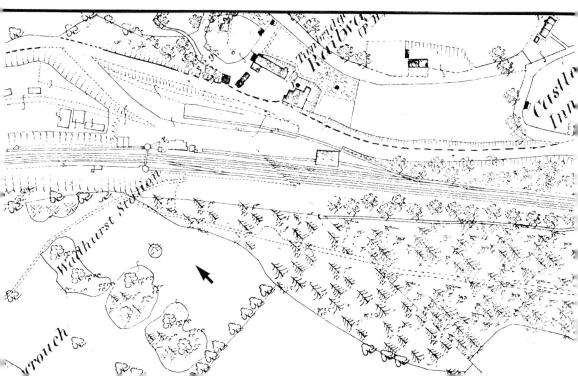

38. An Edwardian postcard captures the atmosphere of the era so well, with most passengers arriving on foot. Beyond the Midland Railway wagon is one with round ends, across which swung a bar for supporting a tarpaulin. (Lens of Sutton)

39. The jib of the 4-ton hand-operated crane is seen in line with the goods shed doorway. An unusual feature of the layout was the separate coal yard, for Messrs. Cheesman and Newington, in front of the Railway Tavern. (Lens of Sutton)

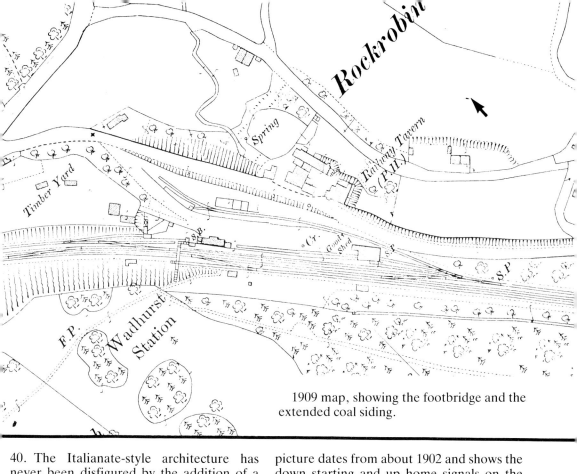

1909 map, showing the footbridge and the extended coal siding.

40. The Italianate-style architecture has never been disfigured by the addition of a canopy on either side of the station. This picture dates from about 1902 and shows the down starting and up home signals on the same bracket. (H.C. Bassett collection)

41. The perfect symmetry of the design was lost when the extension on the right was built, but at least the same styling was perpetuated although the stone pediment of the gable was lost. Station Master Martin rests with his cap on his knee and luggage stands by the roader's shed. This was used for goods arriving or being despatched by van or passenger trains. (H.C. Bassett collection)

42. The antiquated platelayers' transport was photographed in August 1949, during a tea break. It was nick-named by its users *The Spider*. (D. Cullum)

43. An LCGB railtour, headed by class D1 no. 31749 and class L1 no. 31786, returns from a visit to Tenterden on 11th June 1961, on the occasion of the withdrawal of freight services and total closure of the former Kent and East Sussex Railway. The dock sidings can be seen on the left. (S.C. Nash)

44. The signal box was supplied by Duttons in 1893 and replaced an earlier smaller structure. A photograph from January 1984 shows many of the levers out of use and painted white. The goods yard had closed in 1962 and colour lights had come into use in June 1957.

The box closed on 19th April 1986 and was carefully dismantled in March 1987. It was then transported to Northiam for use on the proposed K & ESR extension.
(P.G. Barnes)

45. Chipman's weed killing train runs south, wrong line, on 27th April 1985 as engineers occupy the down line for electrification work. Dr. Beeching proposed closure of this station and could not forsee it as the busiest intermediate station on the route, with an income of around £¾M in 1985.
(P.G. Barnes)

46. The long up siding accommodated the Royal Train on 6th May 1986, whilst the Queen Mother had lunch. Her visit was in connection with the formal introduction of electrified services. The bridge in the distance is an aqueduct carrying one of the headwaters of the River Teise and beyond it is Wadhurst Tunnel. (J. Scrace)

STONEGATE

47. Opened with the line as Withernden, the station was named Ticehurst Road from December 1851 until June 1947. Looking north, we see the "Roader" shed behind the station master and the one-ton crane in front of the goods shed. (Lens of Sutton)

48. The signal box, seen on the left of the previous view, was retained as a porter's room when this larger box came into use in May 1893. The latter had 16 levers and remained in use until 11th May 1984. The goods train has been shunted into the up siding to allow a passenger service to pass it. (H.C. Bassett collection)

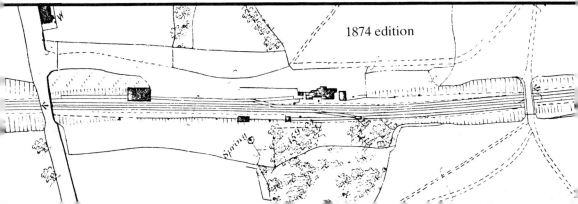

1874 edition

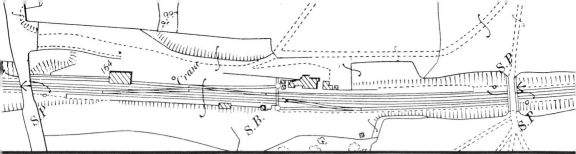

The 1898 map shows an additional siding and two wagon turntables with a line joining them. The latter features were common on the SER and facilitated horse and carriage traffic, which had to move between the back of passenger trains and the loading dock. The crossover was invariably located with the passenger foot crossing, between the ends of the staggered platforms. This staggering made it convenient for transfer of such traffic and safer for passengers to cross the running lines.

49. The goods yard closed in 1961, ten years after this photograph was taken. Goods inward included up to 300 tons of coal per month for Lavenders; cattle from Ashford Market and agricultural machinery for the nearby SCATS depot. Goods outward mainly originated from the farms – hops, apples and notably milk. 18,970 milk churns were despatched in the peak year of 1929 but, by 1935, road transport took them all. (D. Cullum)

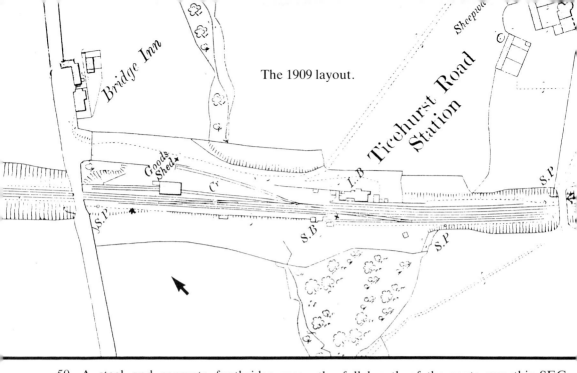

The 1909 layout.

50. A steel and concrete footbridge was erected on 29th July 1985 and the platforms reconstructed in readiness for electrification. The first train of normal width coaches to run the full length of the route was this SEG special on 15th March 1986, which was hauled by no. 50025 *Invincible*. (S.C. Nash)

51. Power was switched on as far as Robertsbridge on 3rd April 1986 and a trial run was made by this train which included two electric driving trailers, mobile test car *Mars* and electro-diesel no. 73128. The footbridge bounces considerably under the weight of a single passenger! (D. Mason)

52. All the stations on the line were extensively renovated prior to electrification and would take a prize for the best restored *series* of stations anywhere. Jack Pennells cared for the station and its passengers from 1944 until 1984, to be succeeded unusually by his youngest daughter. (V. Mitchell)

ETCHINGHAM

53. This is another Gothic style station and is seen prior to the laying of the track. The bay window was replaced by a door, leading to the booking hall and, in 1914, a very generous canopy was added. (Hastings Museum)

The building on the right of the main road on this 1873 map was the Eagle Inn.

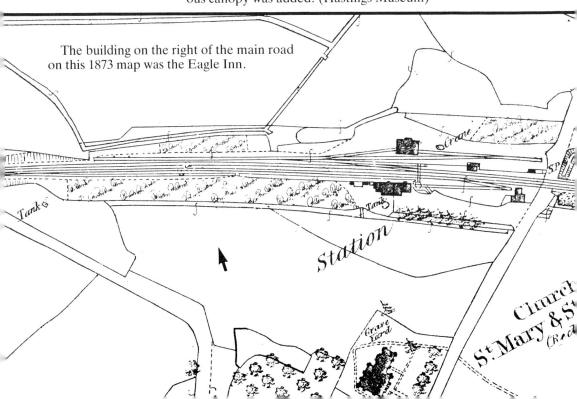

54. Access to the up siding and the goods yard was controlled by the ground frame in the foreground. This is the first station on the line to be close to the village after which it is named, the church being at the end of the main street. (Lens of Sutton)

55. On the left of this picture we see the down platform canopy and the elegant station house. Alas, both have been demolished. The road has been widened and is now the A265 between Heathfield and Hurst Green. (Lens of Sutton)

56. A 1951 view shows the signal box which ceased to be a block post on 29th September 1985, but which continued to be manned during the hours of business of the nearby timber merchants, automatic lifting barriers being a potential hazard to turning timber lorries. (D. Cullum)

57. Schools class *Stowe*, now preserved on the Bluebell Railway, runs north in 1960 and passes the Gents which appears to have been created from the original down waiting shelter. The cottage at the next level crossing to the north (Crowhurst Bridge – named after the bridge over the River Rother) was destroyed by a German V1 rocket on 20th July 1944. (Prof. H.P. White)

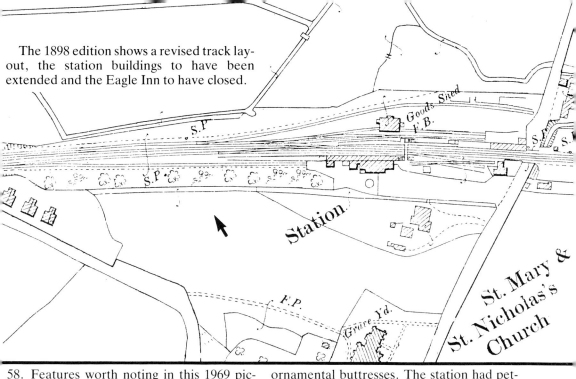

The 1898 edition shows a revised track layout, the station buildings to have been extended and the Eagle Inn to have closed.

58. Features worth noting in this 1969 picture are the exceptionally generous depth of the platform canopy, the light stone quoins and the dainty projecting porch with delicate ornamental buttresses. The station had petrol gas illumination until about 1942 when the plant blew up, injuring Porter Les Pavey. (J. Scrace)

ROBERTSBRIDGE

59. In 1900 Robertsbridge became the junction for the Rother Valley Railway. By 1904, this line had become the Kent and East Sussex Railway and had reached Tenterden. Their train of saloon coaches and an ex-LBSCR 'Terrier' 0–6–0 are seen being loaded in the bay platform. (Lens of Sutton)

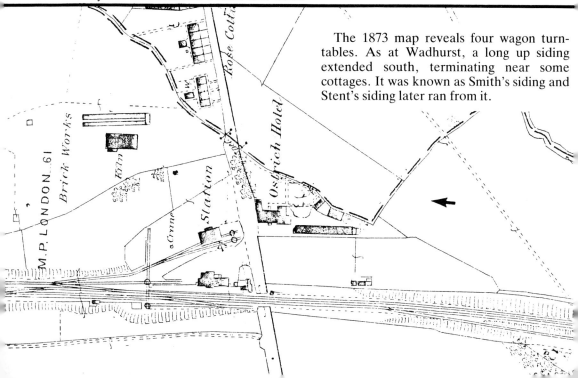

The 1873 map reveals four wagon turntables. As at Wadhurst, a long up siding extended south, terminating near some cottages. It was known as Smith's siding and Stent's siding later ran from it.

60. There have been many enthusiastic station gardeners but few have erected a glasshouse on the platform. The extension of the up platform is obvious – the down platform was extended to accommodate the footbridge. (Lens of Sutton)

61. The K&ESR used petrol-driven railcars as an economy measure for many years. These Ford cars were photographed in the bay platform on 14th March 1931. They were unpopular with the few remaining passengers using the line by then, owing to noise, vibration and smell. (H.C. Casserley)

62. A Terrier stands with a wagon on the
Tenterden branch and a class Q1 stands by
the up water column as three men struggle to
complete the movement of the crossover. BR

gave the former K & ESR signal box, seen on the right, the description of 'Robertsbridge A'. (F. Winding)

63. "The South Eastern Limited" was the last train over the Tenterden and Hawkhurst branches. It ran on the 11th June 1961, originating from Victoria and is pictured in this album returning thereto at Wadhurst. The train engine is class D1 no. 31749 and the pilot is H class no. 31308. (C.R.L. Coles)

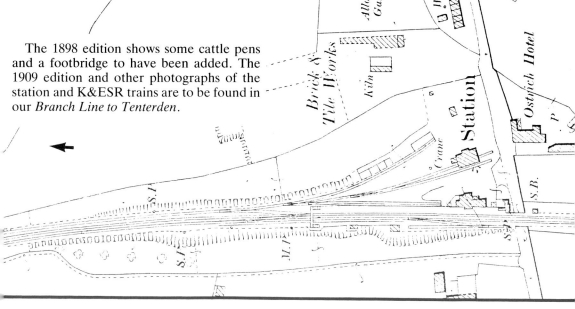

The 1898 edition shows some cattle pens and a footbridge to have been added. The 1909 edition and other photographs of the station and K&ESR trains are to be found in our *Branch Line to Tenterden*.

64. A scheme to preserve part of the K & ESR came to fruition and steam trains now operate regularly at the Tenterden end of the branch. Stock is seen arriving for preservation on 19th September 1964, the Pullman cars destined eventually to provide the popular 'Wine and Dine' service on the line. In the background is the 4-ton crane and the goods shed, the latter becoming a wood stove centre. (S.C. Nash)

65. The coupled or fenestrated chimney stacks of the Italianate station are just visible in this 1969 view. The signal box was converted to panel operation and was the only intermediate one to survive the electrification scheme. (J. Scrace)

66. This photograph was taken on 15th March 1986, from the new footbridge which had been erected in the previous July. Its predecesssor was destined for Northiam on the K & ESR. The 12.33 from Hastings is running 'wrong line' due to engineering work. The crossing gates had been replaced by lifting barriers controlled from the panel box. (J. Scrace)

67. At the south end of Mountfield Tunnel the line curves sharply east and exchange sidings are located here, on the up side, for the gypsum traffic. Barclay 0–6–0ST *Kemp* is seen shunting coal for the works on 25th September 1954, steam operation ceasing in 1967. (D. Cullum)

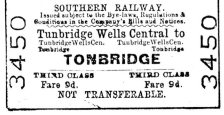

MOUNTFIELD SIDINGS

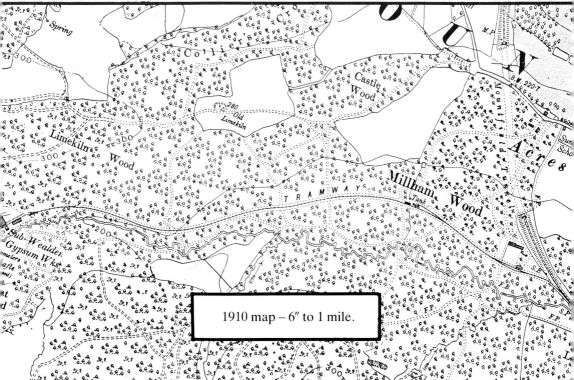

1910 map – 6″ to 1 mile.

68. The Sub-Wealden Gypsum Co. started mining in 1876 and laid a one mile long branch from the main line. A vertical shaft, about 150ft deep, was sunk and another followed later. The head gear was similar to that used above coal mines and both can be seen near the lower corners of this photograph. In 1945, an adit was constructed which allowed 2ft, gauge wagons to descend to about 300ft below ground level, haulage being by steel rope. The inclined plane leading to the adit is just above right centre. Wagons loaded with rock entered sheds and the discharged material was sent by conveyor in two directions as required. Some would be sent to the hopper at the top of the picture for loading into BR wagons, for despatch to various cement works. Other rock would be crushed and conveyed to the kilns, in the lower left quarter of the view, for calcining and removal of all moisture. The resulting plaster would then be loaded into company wagons from the hopper in the centre of the foreground, for transport about ½ mile to the bagging plant, which was located near the engine shed. These coal-fired kilns were demolished in 1967, and in 1973 a plaster board works was established. The head gear has been removed but the shafts retained for ventilation purposes. Only a single standard gauge track remains, along which a Thomas Hill "Vanguard" diesel-electric 0–4–0 hauls a rake of empty wagons and then propels them under the hopper for loading with unprocessed rock, destined for the North-fleet cement works. In 1966, over 400,000 tons of gypsum was transported by rail and twenty years later 3 or 4 trains per week were still running, carrying about 750 tons per trip. All finished products are despatched by road. (Author's collection)

South Eastern and Chatham Railway.

———•———

Local Single Journey Ticket.

No. **I 8701**

_3rd_ **Class.**

_25_ day of _Apl_ 190_8_

From _Ashurst_

To _Tunbridge Wells_

Via _____

Fare Paid ____ 1/8½ _____

_____ Booking Clerk.

COUNTERFOIL.

69. In 1963, a new mine was opened near Brightling and is now the sole source of high grade gypsum for white plaster in the South of England (another mine is located near Carlisle). It is worked to a depth of 850ft by the pillar and stall method, the best of the four seams being up to 14ft thick. To transport the rock to the works at Mountfield, a 3½ mile long aerial ropeway was constructed. This view is from one of the road bridges under which it passes. These pylons are below average in height for that reason – some are 80ft high. The ropeway is likely to be replaced by a conveyor belt in the near future, ending an unusual chapter in Sussex transport history. (D. Cullum)

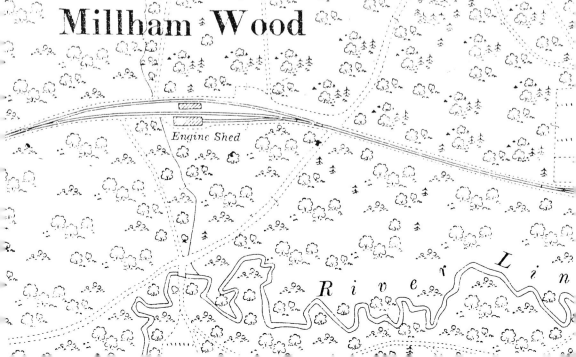

Millham Wood

Engine Shed

River Lin

70. A glimpse from an up train in July 1986, shows the commencement of the mile long branch to the gypsum mines and the tasteful bungalow-like sub-stations erected at various locations on the route during electrification. What a contrast to the pre-war structures which disfigure the countryside elsewhere. (V. Mitchell)

1930 edition, showing a single exchange siding.
Three more were added later.

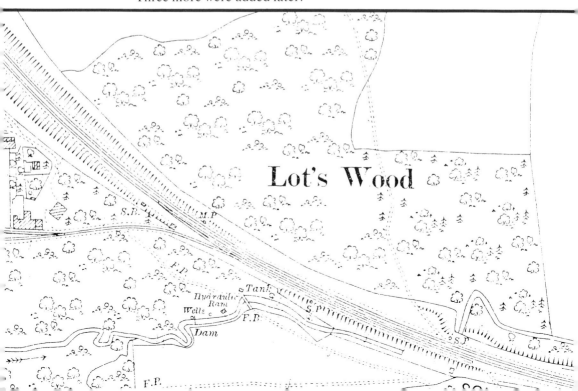

Lot's Wood

MOUNTFIELD HALT

71. The halt was in use from 1923 until 1969 and was ¾ mile east of the gypsum sidings, being adjacent to the crossing over the then A21 London to Hastings road. Here we look west in September 1954, the line continuing to curve behind us to regain a southerly course. (D. Cullum)

047

S. E. & C. R. (SEE BACK

Available for 6 Months

Charing Cross to

ROBERTSBRIDGE

T] First Class 14/8

S. E. & C. R.
Available Day of issue
ONLY. (SEE BACK

Robertsbridge to

CHARING CROSS

14/8 First Class [T

047

SOUTHERN RAILWAY.
PULLMAN CAR TICKET.
Available for one journey on day
of issue only, when accompanied by
First Class Railway Ticket.

Hastings to
LONDON
TWO SHILLINGS.
FOR CONDITIONS SEE BACK.

72. Schools class no. 30930 *Radley*, with a wide pattern chimney, shakes the oil lamp glasses as it tears towards Hastings on 22nd June 1957, with the usual one Pullman car in the formation. (E. Wilmshurst)

73. Tickets were issued from this small hut attached to the crossing keeper's house which was on the opposite side of the busy main road to the platforms. Wicket gates were a less common feature at hand worked crossings. (D. Cullum collection)

74. An engraving from 1852 shows the west facade in fine detail and emphasises the ecclesiastical style windows which were probably intended to appear superior to those in the then ruinous Battle Abbey. The latter was extensively rebuilt as a residence four years later. (Hastings Museum)

76. Looking from the Hastings Road bridge we see a hard-working locomotive entering the down platform. To the right of the smoke is 'No. 2 Cabin', which survived into the 1930s. The SECR preferred *cabin* to *signal box*. (Lens of Sutton)

75. The belfry adds dignity and the climbing plants trained up the fine stonework give a rustic charm to this unique building. This photograph is one of our earliest, dating from 1872, and shows the primitive signalling of that period. (Lens of Sutton)

A faded copy of the 1873 edition shows a layout which changed remarkably little in the ensuing century.

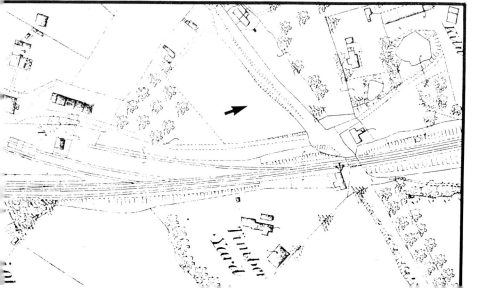

77. Looking south in 1954, we notice that the tall signal post, with co-acting signals, has gone. A similar view in 1987 would show that almost everything else has gone also! A tiny glass 'bus shelter' is provided for passengers. (D. Cullum)

78. Fortunately little has changed since this and the next photograph were taken in 1955. Although the canopy detracts from Tress' original concept, it was fitted with a complementary valance. Look for the charming trefoil window and the ornate ridge tiles. (Prof. H.P. White)

79. The twin arches on substantial columns
guard the doorway to the booking hall which
looks more like a banqueting hall with its fine
timbered ceiling and hooded fireplace. The
battle of 1066 was fought about ½ mile west
of the station. (Prof. H.P. White)

80. Looking north from the footbridge in 1954, the jib of the crane is visible above the busy goods yard. The refuge siding on the right was sometimes used to store gypsum wagons when the Mountfield sidings were congested. (D. Cullum)

81. By 1969 the dock on the left was little used but the station lighting had been modernised. In 1987, T.C. Blackman & Son, the coal merchants, still occupied the northern part of the former goods yard. (J. Scrace)

82. Another 1969 photograph shows Marley Lane crossing, visible in the background of the two previous views. Originally No. 1 Cabin, this signal box was retained until 22nd March 1986, since when the crossing has been supervised by CCTV from Bo-Peep Junction. Note the less common sash windows. (J. Scrace)

CROWHURST

83. This 1955 view shows the relatively plain exterior, when compared with the other stations on the route, that the SECR provided when the branch opened on 1st June 1902. There had been no station here previously. The company had to construct a ½ mile long approach road from Crowhurst Church. (Prof. H.P. White)

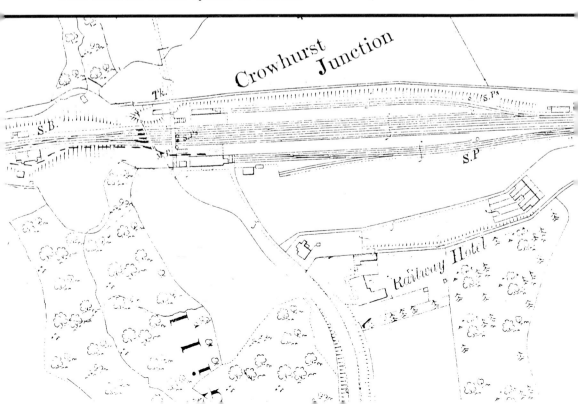

84. All the photographs of this station, except the last, were taken in the mid-1950s, in the hey-day of steam hauled holiday traffic. As with many junction stations, the facilities provided were grossly in excess of what was justified for the small local community. Four cottages for railway staff are on the right. (D. Cullum)

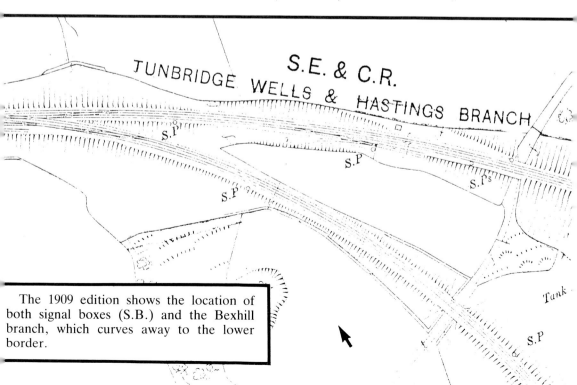

S.E. & C.R.

TUNBRIDGE WELLS & HASTINGS BRANCH

The 1909 edition shows the location of both signal boxes (S.B.) and the Bexhill branch, which curves away to the lower border.

85. A view north from No. 2 Box shows the two bay platforms and the complexity of the signalling. Trains from the branch arrived in the up bay and departed from the down bay, on the right. (D. Cullum).

86. Schools class no. 30928 *Stowe*, now a favourite on the Bluebell line, belches black smoke under the footbridge whilst a lady waits for it to pass. No. 1 Box was situated to the right of the crossover and had been latterly only manned twice a day, by a porter/signalman, for the passage of two trains. It was closed on 9th December 1951. (J. Turley)

87. The branch train arrives behind II class no. 31162, whilst a spare push-pull set stands in the siding. At peak times, the locomotive could be seen sandwiched between two pairs of coaches and the driver would then never travel on the engine. (P. Hay)

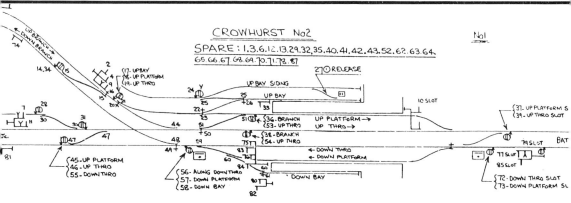

88. The main track layout was similar to that at Ashford prior to electrification, but here there were only two short goods sidings. A wagon of coal arrived from time to time for the solitary local coalman. The structure on the right once carried the tank for the locomotive water supply. A closer view of the signal box is to be found in picture no. 117 in *Steaming through East Sussex*.
(N. Rose collection)

89. Schools class no. 30903 *Charterhouse* approaches with the 1.02 pm from Charing Cross as H class no. 31520 blows off in the bay, ready to propel the branch train to Bexhill West, as soon as the Hastings train has left. This view would now only show a footbridge and a small glass shelter.
(E. Wilmshurst)

90. A 1986 photograph of the up side shows that only a small outbuilding, once used as a lamp room, has been retained for use as a booking office. It was seen earlier, to the left of the exterior view of the station, which was otherwise razed to the ground in November 1984. (V. Mitchell)

91. Class Q1 no. 33028 is seen running past Crowhurst Park siding on 11th May 1957. It is to be found on the 1909 map (under the word *HASTINGS*) and pre-dates the station by at least 25 years. (D. Cullum)

92. *St. Leonards* was one of seven locomotives used to move 300,000 cu.yds. of earth during the construction of the 4½ mile long branch. Temporary structures, of the type illustrated here, were used during the building of many of the 16 bridges on the route. (Hastings Museum)

PASSENGER SERVICES

	Weekdays	Sundays
1910	20	6
1922	20	10
1924	16	9
1938	19	15
1942	9	7
1948	15	8
1956	18	9
1958	22	22
1964	22	–

Prior to World War II, there were some through trains or through coaches but in the last years of steam the only through working was a school train to Etchingham. The coaches were left there overnight. Bo-Peep Tunnel was closed from 27th November 1949 until 5th June 1950 during which period the branch assumed main line status, with most London trains terminating at Bexhill West.

93. The main engineering feature of the branch was the 17-arch Filsham Viaduct, also known as Sidley or Crowhurst Viaduct. It is pictured here on 22nd April 1950, as no. 30939 *Leatherhead*, the last of the Schools class, passes over it with the 2.10 pm Bexhill West to Charing Cross train. (S.C. Nash)

94. Bexhill West had ample sidings in which to berth empty coaches of special trains. These are from a Hop-pickers Friend's Special and are seen returning to Bodiam on 23rd Septmber 1956, hauled by two Terriers, nos. 32636 and 32678. Behind the camera is Adams Farm, where an 18″ gauge tramway ran for 500yds to one of the Hastings Corporation's waterworks. It was hand worked and in use from about 1900 to 1950. (S.C. Nash)

95. The 417yd long viaduct was constructed in 1898-1900 and consumed over nine million bricks. The 70 ft high arches made a spectacular descent on 23rd May 1969. (J. Burke)

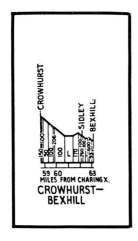

CROWHURST

SIDLEY

BEXHILL

150 100
206
100
L
NO 100
500

59 60   63
MILES FROM CHARING X.
CROWHURST—
BEXHILL

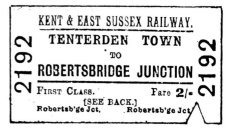

KENT & EAST SUSSEX RAILWAY.
TENTERDEN   TOWN
TO
ROBERTSBRIDGE JUNCTION
First Class.   Fare 2/-
[SEE BACK.]
Robertsb'ge Jct.   Robertsb'ge Jct.
2192   2192

SIDLEY

96. The only intermediate station on the branch had its platforms in a cutting (look for the lamps) and its offices at road level. Oppo- site the latter is the Pelham Hotel, which was built at about the same time. (Lens of Sutton)

The 1909 maps shows the lines to Bexhill on the left and Crowhurst on the right. The location of the 1½ ton crane is also shown.

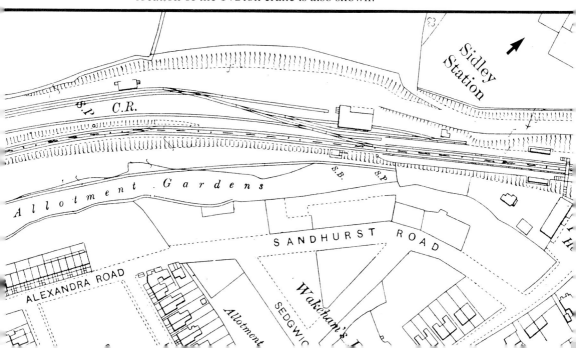

97. The substantial goods shed and part of the extensive coal yard are visible in this photograph, taken on 22nd April 1950. The locomotive is class D no. 31477 which is at the head of the 11.40 am Tonbridge to Bexhill West. (S.C. Nash)

98. A smart push-pull unit proceeds towards Bexhill West ahead of no. 31162 on 25th May 1957. The signal box with the attractive barge boards had 16 levers in use and 4 spare. The yard is now used as a council depot. (P. Hay)

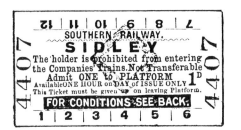

99. DEMUs were introduced to the branch in 1958 and usually one set sufficed for the declining traffic. Sets 2H no. 1120 and 4S no. 1007 were combined on the last day of public services – 14th June 1964. (S.C. Nash)

100. Most of the main building became a club in 1939 and was eventually turned into a garage, only to be later demolished. The ladies room was apparently retained at the high level – the sign is visible in this 1964 view. Tickets were issued from the building on the up platform. (S.C. Nash)

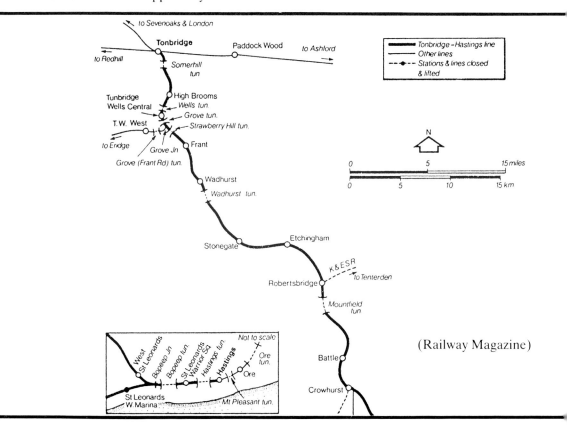

BEXHILL WEST

101. Until 1929, the station was "Bexhill-on-Sea". Four platform faces were provided and 'B' Cabin can be seen at the end of the engine release road. The right hand crossover was later removed but the other remained to the end. (Lens of Sutton)

102. This is the view from 'B' Cabin (or No. 2 Box , as it was often called) on 14th May 1950. Platforms 3 and 4 had been demolished by then but the two-road locomotive shed

can be seen on the extreme left. Standing
outside it is class D3 no. 32388. The gas cylin-
ders in the foreground were for recharging
the Pullman car cooker tanks. (J.J. Smith)

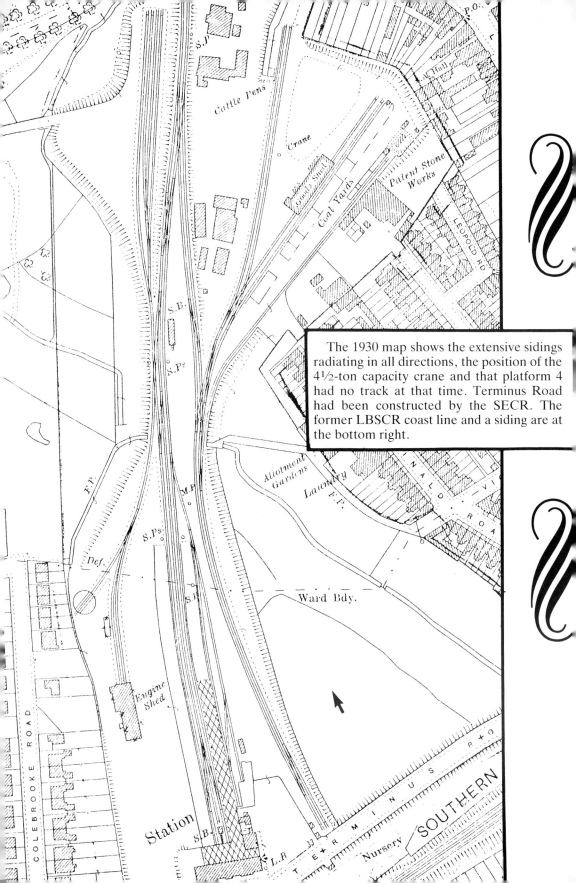

The 1930 map shows the extensive sidings radiating in all directions, the position of the 4½-ton capacity crane and that platform 4 had no track at that time. Terminus Road had been constructed by the SECR. The former LBSCR coast line and a siding are at the bottom right.

103. The palatial No. 1 Box had 48 working levers and 75 spares, at the end of its life. The gas lamps, frayed carpet and kitchen range complete the vintage scene. (J.J. Smith)

104. The gigantic signal box controls a simple shunt movement on 23rd March 1959. A lavish double track connection to the goods yard was provided behind the signal box. The former closed in September 1963. (S.C. Nash)

105. The fireman relaxes after his lonely journey, while the passengers disappear through the barrier. The driver chats with the guard before returning to the footplate of class D3 ex-LBSCR 0–4–4T no. 32384. (J. Turley)

→

106. By 14th July 1963, the station was a scene of dereliction with a crop of weeds under the glassless canopy and defective wagons stored in the grass-filled sidings. A two-coach DEMU waits to depart at 11.44. (E. Wilmshurst)

→

107. The flamboyant exterior was complemented internally by an elegant refreshment room and a booking office that was once described as "reminiscent of a baronial hall with a high beamed roof and a vast fireplace." The building has subsequently served a variety of purposes and is still standing. (C. Hall)

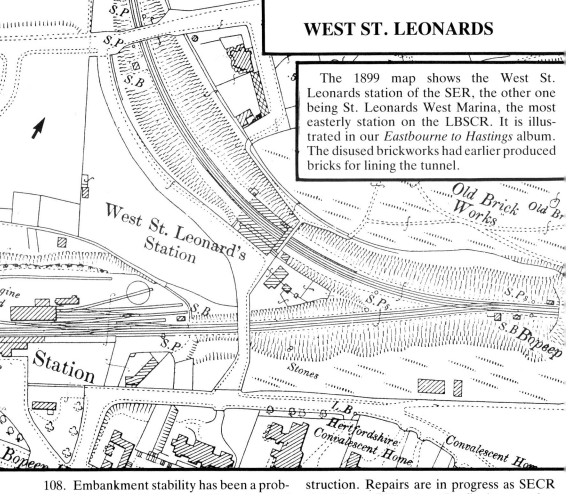

WEST ST. LEONARDS

The 1899 map shows the West St. Leonards station of the SER, the other one being St. Leonards West Marina, the most easterly station on the LBSCR. It is illustrated in our *Eastbourne to Hastings* album. The disused brickworks had earlier produced bricks for lining the tunnel.

108. Embankment stability has been a problem since the line was opened as many of them were built from the sand and clay that caused so much trouble in the tunnel construction. Repairs are in progress as SECR class D no. 741 enters the final curve that leads into the station. (Lens of Sutton)

109. The station was opened in 1887, the same year as Ore. A 1931 view shows two signal boxes at Bo-Peep Junction. The taller one was erected by the SR to replace the two shown on the map. (D. Cullum collection)

110. During the prolonged closure of Bo-Peep tunnel for repairs in 1950, a push-pull service was operated between West St. Leonards and Crowhurst and all main line trains ran into Bexhill West. Ex-LBSCR class D3 no. 32388 was working between two pairs of coaches. (S.C. Nash)

111. The 11.40 from Charing Cross creeps round the curve on 5th June 1975. On electrification the speed limit was raised from 20 to 25 mph. The signal box controls the junction and entry to the St. Leonards depot and carriage washer, which are concealed by trees to the left of the picture. (J. Scrace)

112. The main building is similar to that at Ore and its centenary year coincides with the publication of this book. The platforms have been lengthened to take eight coaches and the old covered footbridge remains in use. (J. Scrace)

British Rail

1966
COUNTRY

Celebrating the First Day o
Electrified Services on the
Hastings Line

VALID FOR ANY JOURNEY BETWEEN TONBRID(
HASTINGS AND INTERMEDIATE STATIONS VIA BATT
ON

SUNDAY, 27 APRIL, 1986   № ˙ 1021

THIS TICKET MAY BE RETAINED AS A SOUVENIR

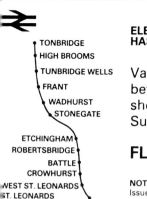

BR 4536/1

ELECTRIFICATION OF THE HASTINGS LINE, MAY 1986

TONBRIDGE
HIGH BROOMS
TUNBRIDGE WELLS
FRANT
WADHURST
STONEGATE
ETCHINGHAM
ROBERTSBRIDGE
BATTLE
CROWHURST
WEST ST. LEONARDS
ST. LEONARDS
WARRIOR SQ.
HASTINGS

Valid for any journey between stations shown on Sunday 27th April 1986

FLAT FARE: 50p

NOT TRANSFERABLE
Issued subject to the regulations and conditions in the publications and notices of the British Railways Board.

113. St. Leonards Depot undertook the maintenance and heavy overhauls of the DEMU fleet for nearly 30 years. Many of the staff felt like shedding a tear when these durable machines were taken out of service, although they still care for a few units for the services via Rye and Oxted. (C. Dadswell)

114. Bunting links the new lamp standards on 6th May 1986 as celebrations begin to launch the new "1066 Electrics". This was the marketing slogan which accompanied the smart new livery. A gala day on 27th April 1986 generated so much traffic that the 50p tickets were exhausted and extra trains had to be summoned from London. (J. Scrace)

ST. LEONARDS WARRIOR SQUARE

115. A gloomy day in February 1952 was not ideal to photograph the arrival of the 12.18 from Cannon Street but it did give the opportunity to record the engineers' possession of the up line for tunnel repairs. The down canopy is also being renovated but it has since been destroyed. (J.J. Smith)

116. A 1957 view towards Hastings shows the well protected platforms and the covered footbridge, which is not restricted to ticket holders. The up platform still has the luxury of refreshment facilities but the Gents has the antiquity of being open to the sky. (D. Cullum)

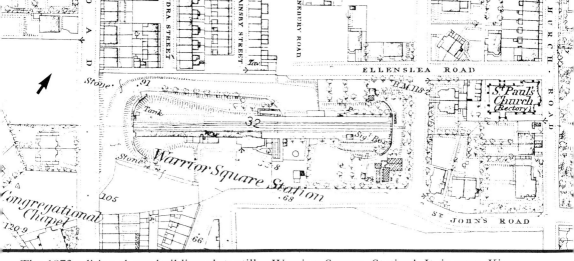

The 1873 edition shows building plots still vacant and Gensing Station Road leading to Warrior Square Station! It is now Kings Road.

117. A 1984 photograph shows the minimal down canopy and the simplified valance on the up one. This is another case of the architect's design being ruined in the interest of passengers in wet weather. The projecting foot boards were an unavoidably ugly feature of this unique slim-line stock.
(J.A.M. Vaughan)

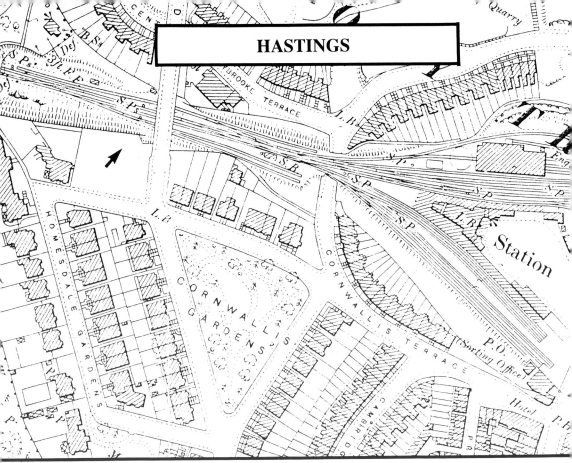

HASTINGS

The 1899 map reveals the awkward and cramped layout created by compromise. A single through platform was available for SER trains and a single roofed platform was provided for terminating LBSCR trains. There was an additional terminal platform with two faces and no roof. There were no engine release crossovers. (Lens of Sutton)

118. The features seen on the map, the SER engine shed and the West Box can all be found in this 1893 picture. Note the white dot instead of a stripe on the signal. (Lens of Sutton)

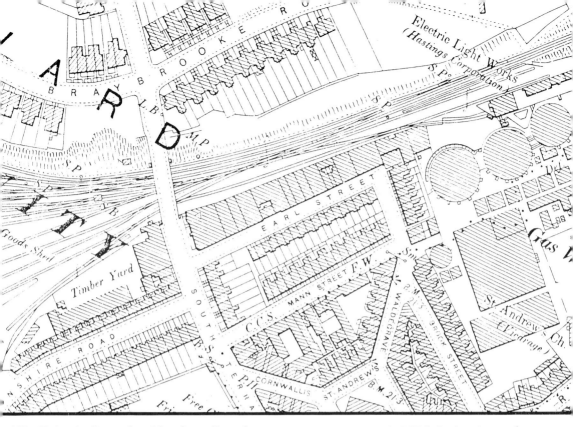

119. Being built on the side of a valley, the station has always suffered from limited carriage berthing space. As a result, sidings were provided at St. Leonards and Ore. Here we see class L no. 31767 bringing in stock from St. Leonards to form the 10.10 am service to Charing Cross on 26th March 1955.

(E. Gamblin)

120. The station was completely rebuilt in 1931 to give two island platforms and much greater operating flexibility. Another advance was electrification via Lewes on 7th July 1935. In 1986, the track at this end of platform 4 (on the right) was severed to allow the construction of level access to the booking hall. The 13.33 leaves platform 3 on 28th August 1985, bound for Charing Cross. Many will miss the unique sound effects – others will be thankful for the quiet comfort of the '1066 Electrics' in which to enjoy this unusual main line, which combines exceptional natural beauty with a complete set of original intermediate stations. (J. Scrace)

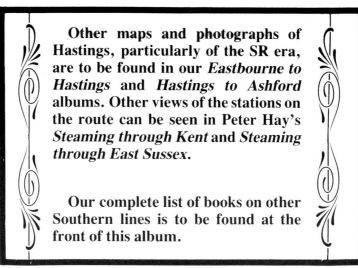

Other maps and photographs of Hastings, particularly of the SR era, are to be found in our *Eastbourne to Hastings* and *Hastings to Ashford* albums. Other views of the stations on the route can be seen in Peter Hay's *Steaming through Kent* and *Steaming through East Sussex*.

Our complete list of books on other Southern lines is to be found at the front of this album.